S0-BZC-420

Fighting a
Battle

By Deborah Murrell

WORLD ALMANAC® LIBRARY

Please visit our web site at: www.garethstevens.com.
For a free color catalog describing Gareth Stevens Publishing's
list of high-quality books call 1-800-542-2595 (USA)
or 1-800-387-3178 (Canada).
Gareth Stevens Publishing's fax: 1-877-542-2596

Library of Congress Cataloging-in-Publication Data

Murrell, Deborah Jane, 1963-
    Fighting a battle / Deborah Murrell.
        p. cm. — (Medieval warfare)
    Includes bibliographical references and index.
    ISBN-13: 978-0-8368-9209-3 (lib. bdg.)
    ISBN-10: 0-8368-9209-7 (lib. bdg.)
    ISBN-13: 978-0-8368-9336-6 (softcover)
    ISBN-10: 0-8368-9336-0 (softcover)
    1. Military art and science—History—Medieval, 500-1500—Juvenile
literature. 2. Crusades—Juvenile literature. I. Title.
U37.M85 2008
909.07—dc22   2008016833

This North American edition first published in 2009 by
World Almanac® Library
An Imprint of Gareth Stevens Publishing
1 Reader's Digest Road
Pleasantville, NY 10570-7000 USA

Copyright © 2009 by Amber Books, Ltd.
Produced by Amber Books Ltd., Bradley's Close
74–77 White Lion Street
London N1 9PF, U.K.

All illustrations © Amber Books, Ltd. except:
AKG Images: 4, 10, 20; Art-Tech/MARS: 3, 6–7; Corbis: 14 (Art Archive);
Mary Evans Picture Library: 21; Topfoto: 19, 22, 27

Amber Project Editor: James Bennett
Amber Designer: Joe Conneally

Gareth Stevens Senior Managing Editor: Lisa M. Herrington
Gareth Stevens Editor: Joann Jovinelly
Gareth Stevens Creative Director: Lisa Donovan
Gareth Stevens Designer: Paul Bodley

Printed in the United States of America

1 2 3 4 5 6 7 8 9 10 09 08

Contents

CHAPTER 1

Fighting on Horseback

Constant warfare defined Europe after the fall of the Roman Empire in A.D. 476. The order and protection provided by Roman armies had ended. Europe became a group of disorganized kingdoms. Each fought one another for land and power. Castles were built to protect **nobles** from outsiders. Better weapons were developed to ward off invaders. The steady fighting lasted 1,000 years, until 1453, when the Hundred Years' War between England and France ended. That time is known as the Middle Ages, or medieval period. At the end of the medieval period, the European countries we know today began to form.

Most people think of medieval knights on horseback when they think about the Middle Ages. However, there is no evidence of people fighting on horseback in northern Europe until the 700s. In medieval England and Scandinavia, nobles traveled to battles on horses, but they originally fought only on foot. Soldiers had to supply their own animals and equipment. Just to own a horse in those days meant that you were very rich. Some historians believe nobles may have considered their horses too valuable to risk in battle. Since few soldiers could afford a horse, those soldiers who had one did not want to lose it in a battle.

▶ CAVALRY BATTLE
This medieval illustration shows Charlemagne's cavalry in 778, armed with spears and swords. They were fighting the **Basque** people of the Pyrenees Mountains in Spain.

Early Tactics on Horseback

Soldiers fighting on horseback are known as **cavalry**. The army of King Charlemagne (SHAR-le-main), ruler of the **Franks**, is thought to be the first medieval army to use cavalry as its main force, in the late 700s.

One of Charlemagne's favorite battle **tactics** involved cavalry. He ordered three or four lines of knights on horseback to charge a line of **infantry**, or foot soldiers. If the infantry withstood the first line's charge and stood its ground, Charlemagne's horsemen turned to the right and to the left. The soldiers then rejoined the cavalry lines at the back, ready to charge again. In this way, there was always a line of cavalry

moving forward. Within a short time, the infantry stopped fighting and fled.

This was the beginning of the cavalry charge, the most feared battle tactic in the Middle Ages. It also led to the beginning of the romantic idea of the armored knight.

In Their Own Words

"The function of knights is … to fight unbelievers, to protect the poor from injuries, to pour out their blood for their brothers, and if need be to lay down their lives."

—John of Salisbury, *Policraticus*, 1159

▼ CAVALRY TACTICS
Charlemagne, king of the Franks, ordered his cavalry to charge in lines. Once the first line had charged, it turned to the left and right, rejoining the lines at the back. The constant attack from soldiers on horseback was terrifying to enemy forces. Charlemagne went on to rule much of western Europe.

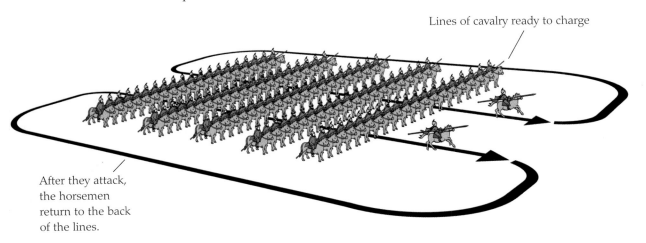

Lines of cavalry ready to charge

After they attack, the horsemen return to the back of the lines.

Cavalry Catches On

By 800, Charlemagne and his successors had conquered a large part of Europe. Other European kingdoms rushed to build cavalry forces because of Charlemagne's success.

One very important change that made cavalry so effective in medieval Europe was the increased use of the stirrup. That was a ring with a flat bottom fixed on a leather strap. Stirrups hung from each side of a horse's saddle. They allowed a horseman to strike heavy blows with a sword or ax without falling.

Stirrups had been used in Asia since ancient times. But Charlemagne was one of the first European leaders to insist that his cavalry use them. Saddles with high fronts and backs also made knights more stable on their horses. Cavalry soon became an important part of all European armies.

Around 200 years later, William of Normandy, in northern France, made excellent use of cavalry to conquer England. He led his Norman knights in cavalry forces and secured a victory over the English at the Battle of Hastings in 1066. William's knights charged the English infantry again and again, until they were defeated. The English king, Harold, was killed, and William was crowned the new King of England.

▼ BAYEUX TAPESTRY

This embroidered cloth, or tapestry, was created to celebrate William of Normandy's victory over King Harold of England in 1066. In it you can see Normans on horseback attacking the English infantry.

Types of Horses

Over time, medieval warriors favored certain horses for their size or speed. By the 1100s, breeders had developed a special horse for mounted warfare. It was called the destrier (DESS-tree-ur). It was larger and stronger than earlier warhorses. That strength helped it to carry a fully armored knight. People understood that an organized cavalry charge could overcome an enemy's infantry. They were soon convinced that mounted knights, despite their small numbers, controlled warfare.

▼ WILLIAM OF NORMANDY'S CAVALRY
Norman horsemen were lightly armored. They wore chain mail made of many tiny metal rings linked together. They also had simple iron helmets. Their long spears and the thundering of their hooves as they charged frightened the English infantry.

Stirrups kept horsemen stable in their saddles. They were able to stand up to deliver blows to the enemy with greater force.

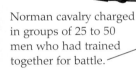
Norman cavalry charged in groups of 25 to 50 men who had trained together for battle.

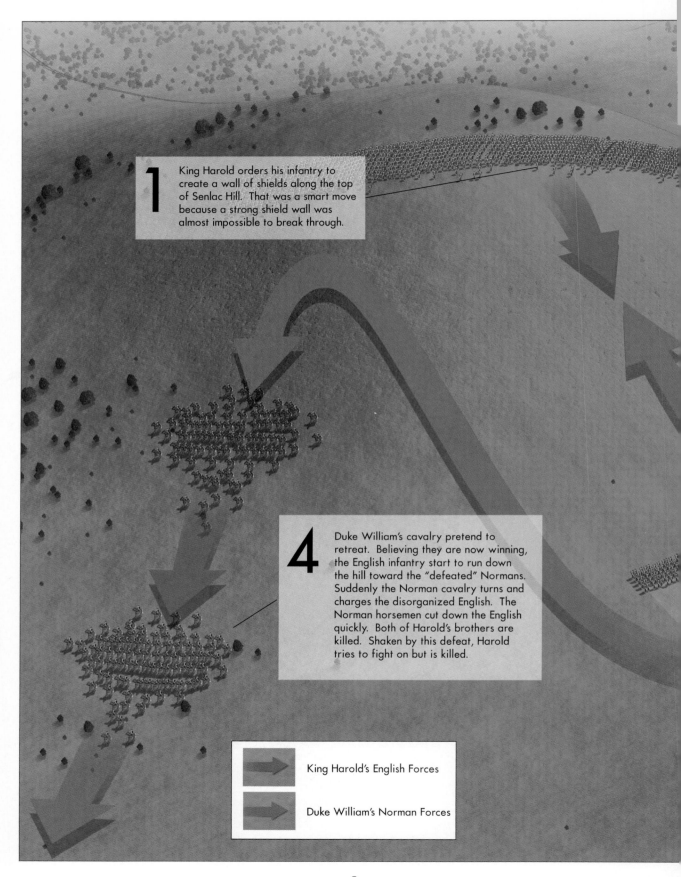

1 King Harold orders his infantry to create a wall of shields along the top of Senlac Hill. That was a smart move because a strong shield wall was almost impossible to break through.

4 Duke William's cavalry pretend to retreat. Believing they are now winning, the English infantry start to run down the hill toward the "defeated" Normans. Suddenly the Norman cavalry turns and charges the disorganized English. The Norman horsemen cut down the English quickly. Both of Harold's brothers are killed. Shaken by this defeat, Harold tries to fight on but is killed.

King Harold's English Forces

Duke William's Norman Forces

2 Duke William's infantry and archers attack first, but they are quickly forced back.

3 The Norman cavalry begins a series of charges up the hill at the English infantry shield wall. The attacks continue for several hours, but the English infantry defend themselves.

The Battle of Hastings
October 14, 1066

The Battle of Hastings is one of the most famous events in English history. Duke William of Normandy was the proud ruler of northern France. He also claimed the throne of England.

When King Edward the Confessor of England died in January 1066, he named Harold Godwinson as the new king. William was outraged. He claimed that before Edward died, the English king had promised him the throne. Not ready to give up, William decided to take England by force. His cavalry was highly trained. King Harold's infantry was in northern England. They had just defeated another army whose leader also claimed England's throne.

When Harold heard of William's invasion, he marched his men, mostly foot soldiers, about 250 miles (402 kilometers) south. They met William's forces at Senlac Hill, near Hastings. They took up position on top of the hill. Unfortunately for Harold's soldiers, William's cavalry tricked them into defeat.

CHAPTER 2

Fighting on Foot

While mounted knights often got the glory, foot soldiers were the core of medieval armies. From archers to soldiers with pikes (long spears) and axes, infantry did most of the fighting. Leadership was important, as medieval foot soldiers often became disorganized. Tactics were also crucial to winning. A strong, organized front line with pikes pointed forward could withstand charging knights.

Pikemen protected archers as they shot their arrows. The foot soldiers also defended knights before they began their charge.

Unlike knights, who came from the noble classes, infantry came from many different backgrounds. Some soldiers were poor.

▼ FOOT SOLDIERS FIGHTING
Foot soldiers in medieval armies fought bravely, often with poor equipment. This image from the 1400s shows a range of infantry weapons.

Swords were used for slashing and stabbing.

Small round shields were thrust at an enemy's face during close combat.

A simple bow was accurate only at close range.

Pole-arms were long-handled spiked axes.

▼ WELSH INFANTRY
These illustrations show what ordinary foot soldiers looked like in the 1300s. They had poor clothing and basic weapons, but this Welsh archer and spearman from Edward I's army were part of a greatly feared fighting force.

Soldiers armed with a 14-foot (4.3-meter) pikes could fight off a cavalry charge.

A round shield provided some defense.

A simple **tunic** gave no protection to the body.

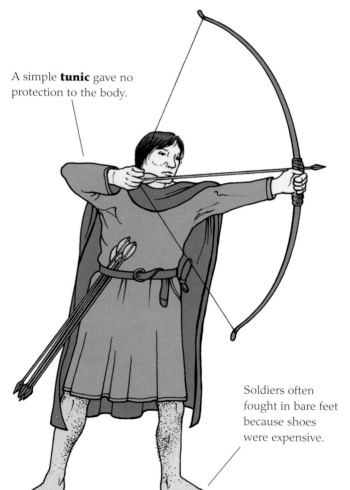

Soldiers often fought in bare feet because shoes were expensive.

They fought with little or no armor. Their only weapons were farm tools. Other soldiers were armed, but few had well-made weapons like knights. Most soldiers fought for only part of the year. They had to go home to farm the land and provide food for their families. Only professional soldiers spent most of their time fighting.

Shields and Tactics

Most infantrymen had a shield. Men in the front line of a battle often formed a shield wall, standing close together with their shields in front. Pikemen held pikes in front of their shields. That usually protected against a cavalry charge because horses were afraid of the pointed weapons. But if just a few of the pikemen lost their nerve and gave way, the whole line would be destroyed. The enemy cavalry could then break through the line. Once that happened, the knights slashed their way among the poorly armored foot soldiers.

Byzantine and Arab Infantry

The Byzantine (Biz-ZAN-tine) Empire ruled much of eastern Europe from its capital, Constantinople (present-day Istanbul, Turkey), for most of the Middle Ages. Byzantine foot soldiers were well-trained.

▶ BYZANTINE INFANTRY
Byzantine infantrymen were among the most dangerous soldiers in the world in the 500s. They had tough armor and well-made weapons. Most important, they had effective tactics and discipline.

Byzantine spearmen planted their spears in the ground at an angle to defend themselves against charging cavalry.

A chain mail coat was often worn over a padded tunic.

A sword was kept in its **sheath** after a battle.

A short, heavy javelin was an Almogavar warrior's main weapon.

A simple leather cap gave little protection.

Byzantine infantry was mainly used for defense. Foot soldiers formed a square that would hold back an enemy. That allowed their own cavalry to charge and surprise or surround the enemy. Muslim Arab armies, who were the Byzantine Empire's main enemy, used a similar approach. Arab infantry, who traveled by camel, also formed walls with blocks of men. The Arab soldiers kneeled on the ground, protected by spears. Within those blocks were safe areas where the cavalry could regroup after an attack.

Mountain Men

The Almogavars, professional fighters from Spain, had a fierce reputation as foot soldiers. They came from the mountains, where horses were of little use in fighting. As the Almogavars went into battle with **javelins** and heavy knives, they cried, "*Aur! Aur! Desperta Ferra!*" which meant "Listen! Listen! The iron awakes!"

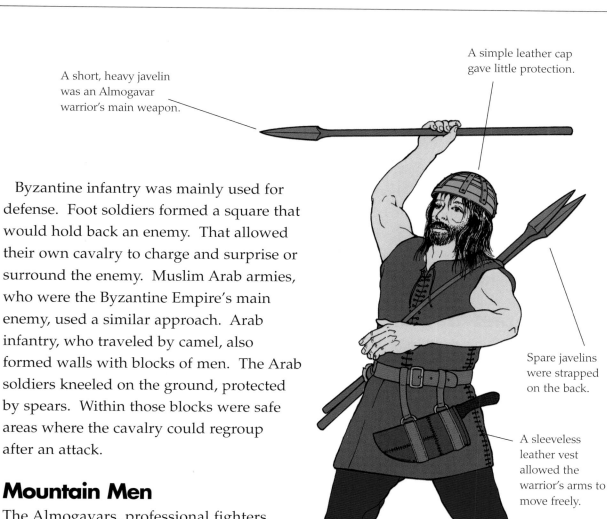

Spare javelins were strapped on the back.

A sleeveless leather vest allowed the warrior's arms to move freely.

▲ AN ALMOGAVAR WARRIOR
Almogavar soliders originally came from Spain, but they fought all over Europe for money. Their knives were similar to meat cleavers. They could cut through a man's leg in one blow. This knife is stored in a leather sheath for safety.

CHAPTER 3

Battle Tactics

Planning a battle in the Middle Ages was quite different from planning a battle today. For one thing, medieval leaders didn't have much information. There were few maps available, and they were often incorrect. Leaders had to ask local villagers where enemies were hiding. Few people could be trusted to tell the truth.

Command and Control

If the leader believed he could trust the villagers, he might call his advisers together. The advisers met to plan their attack. Leaders sent **heralds** to give their commanders instructions. Once all the troops were assembled, commanders divided them into groups, or divisions. Each division was led by a noble, because no one would take orders from someone of lower rank.

Planning and Tactics

Medieval military leaders used different fighting tactics depending on whom they were fighting. They had to also consider the kind of ground on which they were fighting. Different sites were used in different ways. Leaders knew how to best

▼ PLANNING A SIEGE
A siege was when an army surrounded a castle or city to try to capture it. Invaders would attempt to knock down castle walls or starve out the defenders. Planning how to carry out a siege was important. Besieging a city was expensive and might last for years.

The position of an army's archers and the bows they used could sometimes decide a battle. The English **longbows** pictured here could shoot farther than **crossbows**. That meant that longbowmen could be positioned farther away from the enemy. Longbowmen could shoot at the enemy while remaining out of range of their arrows.

Stakes were planted into the ground to protect archers from an enemy cavalry charge.

use steep hillsides, muddy swamps, or flat plains to their advantage. Battlefield communication was very slow in medieval times. The tactics of many battles were planned in advance. Once on a battlefield, leaders used **scouts** on horseback to further instruct soldiers. The scouts took any new messages to the troops. Commanders also used trumpets to give signals.

Hide and Seek

One well-used tactic on the medieval battlefield was to hide some soldiers. The tactic fooled the enemy about the size of the army it was fighting. Commanders often hid troops in wooded areas or behind hills. Then, on a signal, the hidden soldiers burst out to surprise the enemy. The tactic was sometimes useful for turning the tide of battle.

Surrounding an enemy was also a common tactic. Pretending to withdraw and then suddenly attacking was another. In 1213 at the battle of Muret in France, a large army attempted to capture the town. The town's defender, Simon de Montfort, ordered his cavalry to pretend to retreat. When the attackers followed, Montfort's cavalry quickly defeated them. As a result, Montfort's men held the town.

To be successful, medieval battles needed good planning, timing, and control. Leaders relied on their commanders to follow the battle plan. Once the battle started, however, even the best-laid plans could fall apart.

DID YOU KNOW?

Medieval kings were also military leaders. They went into battle with their armies and were sometimes killed on the battlefield.

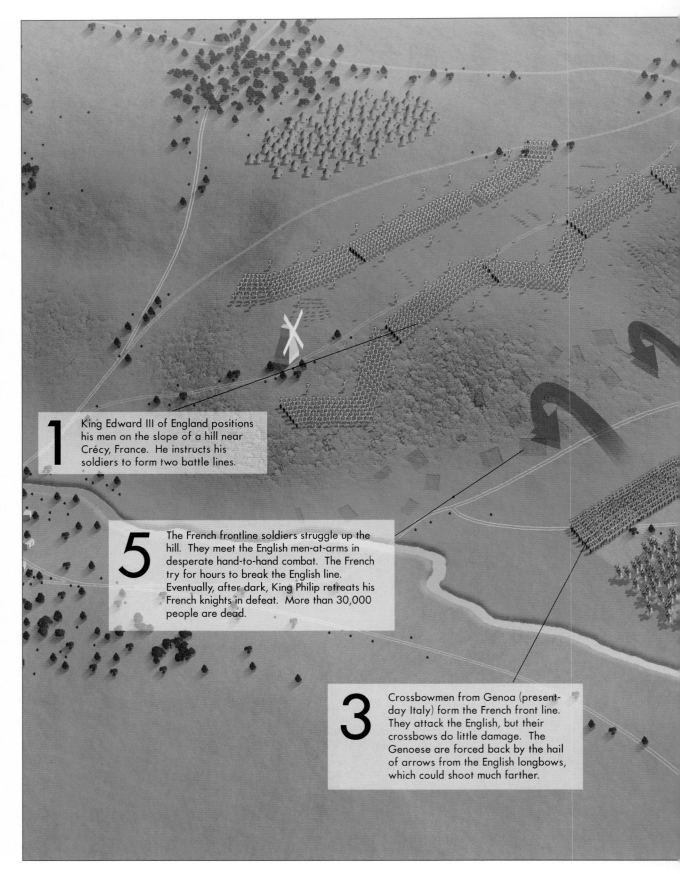

1 King Edward III of England positions his men on the slope of a hill near Crécy, France. He instructs his soldiers to form two battle lines.

5 The French frontline soldiers struggle up the hill. They meet the English men-at-arms in desperate hand-to-hand combat. The French try for hours to break the English line. Eventually, after dark, King Philip retreats his French knights in defeat. More than 30,000 people are dead.

3 Crossbowmen from Genoa (present-day Italy) form the French front line. They attack the English, but their crossbows do little damage. The Genoese are forced back by the hail of arrows from the English longbows, which could shoot much farther.

2 English soldiers dig pits at the foot of the hill. They want to make it harder for the French cavalry to charge at them.

4 The French knights shove the archers aside and mount an attack. They are disorganized and do not have a strong commander. They struggle through the English ditches. Many of their horses are killed by longbow arrows.

The Battle of Crécy
August 26, 1346

In 1337, King Edward III of England claimed he had a right to the French crown. He started the Hundred Years' War (which actually lasted 116 years). In 1346, Edward invaded Normandy in northern France. His soldiers met with French forces near Crécy (CRAY-sea).

Edward chose to fight on an open piece of farmland. There was a ridge behind his soldiers and forests to both their sides. His men took over a windmill so they could have a good view of the battlefield. Edward's army numbered about 16,000 men, including 7,000 archers. The French forces and their **allies** were much larger — about 80,000, most of whom were knights on horseback.

Edward won an important battle at Crécy. He showed how an organized force of **men-at-arms** and archers could beat a much larger force of mounted knights by using clever tactics.

CHAPTER 4

Fighting in the Crusades

The Crusades were a long series of wars fought during the Middle Ages. They lasted roughly 250 years, and were among the bloodiest battles of the period. The battles were fought mainly between Christians and Muslims in Jerusalem and the Holy Land, the region known today as the Middle East. For centuries, the Muslim rulers of the Holy Land had allowed Christian **pilgrims** to travel there to pray. But in the 1000s, new Muslim rulers, the Seljuk Turks, took over. They attacked Christian pilgrims. In response, Pope Urban II in 1095 ordered a crusade of Christian knights to recapture Jerusalem for Christianity.

▼ SELJUK TURK HORSEMAN
The Seljuk Turks were originally from the **steppes** of central Asia. Warriors from this region were excellent horseback riders. This Seljuk horse archer would have been a deadly enemy for an untrained Crusader.

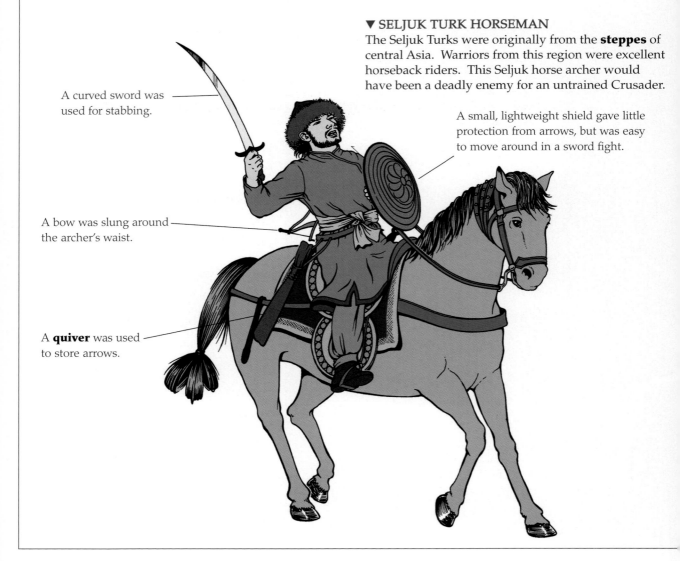

A curved sword was used for stabbing.

A small, lightweight shield gave little protection from arrows, but was easy to move around in a sword fight.

A bow was slung around the archer's waist.

A **quiver** was used to store arrows.

▼ PETER THE HERMIT

The Christians who marched to the Holy Land in the 1090s were encouraged by the preaching of monks and other holy men. The most important of these monks was Peter the Hermit. He is shown here leading knights into battle, but he rarely fought. Instead, he convinced Christian **peasants** to go to the Holy Land to fight the Seljuk Turks. Untrained and unarmed, the Christians were slaughtered by the first Seljuk army they met.

DID YOU KNOW?

The Crusaders learned to use carrier pigeons from the Seljuk Turks. Messages were fixed to the pigeon's tail or under its wing.

19

Crusader Battles

In May 1097, a huge army of Crusaders landed in the Holy Land. Led by nobles from different areas of Europe, they besieged the Seljuk capital city of Nicaea (Ny-SEE-uh), now in present-day Turkey. After capturing the city, they defeated the Seljuk army at Dorylaeum (DORRY-lay-um). The victorious Crusaders then marched toward Antioch (ANTI-ock).

The conditions were harsh. The Crusaders had little food and water. Many of their horses died. Some knights gave up and went home. But most carried on, finally reaching Antioch in October 1097. They surrounded the city and, by **bribing** one of its defenders, broke in and took control. The Muslim forces attempted to retake Antioch. The Crusaders struggled on and defended it successfully.

Jerusalem Captured

In 1099, the Crusaders reached the holy city of Jerusalem and slaughtered its Muslim population. Christians had achieved their goal of taking Jerusalem from the Muslims.

The Crusaders held Jerusalem and parts of the Holy Land for nearly 100 years. In 1187, Saladin, the Muslim ruler of Egypt, united Muslim forces in the Holy Land under his rule and recaptured Jerusalem. Crusaders kept coming to the Holy Land and kept

fighting. But gradually all the Crusaders'
territory was recaptured by Muslim armies.
The last Crusader stronghold was lost in
1291, when the fortified city of Acre, now in
present-day Israel, fell to Muslim forces.

▼ KRAK DES CHEVALIERS, SYRIA

Captured from Muslim forces and rebuilt by the Crusaders, this is
Krak des Chevaliers (CRAK day SHEV-al-ee-ay) in present-day
Syria. It was the largest Crusader fortress in the Holy Land. In
1271, the castle was recaptured by Muslim attackers after they
tricked its defenders into surrendering.

CHAPTER 5

War at Sea

Keeping a standing navy ready to fight was too expensive. To cut costs, rulers instead hired or seized merchant ships when they needed to move troops.

Greek Fire

Greek fire was the most dangerous weapon in the Middle Ages. It was an oil-based substance that could be shot from a ship like a flamethrower. When it reached its target, it burst into flames, and was almost impossible to put out. Greek fire even burned on water. Its ingredients were a secret. Even today, we do not know what they were.

Blazing Ships

During the early Middle Ages, the Byzantine emperor Justinian built a standing navy. In 673, when Muslims attacked Constantinople, the Byzantine capital, Justinian's navy was ready to meet them. The Byzantine fleet sailed out of the city's harbor, pelting the Muslim ships with Greek fire. The ships burned and the shocked Muslims retreated or were drowned. A Muslim navy was defeated a second time when they tried to take Constantinople again in 717.

◄ A PITCHED BATTLE AT SEA
This illustration shows a naval battle between English and French forces during the Hundred Years' War. Ships were so valuable that many naval battles were fought by armored soldiers who tried to board and capture each others' ships.

▼ A NAVAL SIEGE TOWER

When attacking a walled city or castle on the coast, medieval forces built siege towers on the front of their ships. The towers were the same as those used on land. They allowed soldiers to reach the tops of castle walls.

Archers used a platform at the top of the ship's mast.

A ramp protected the soldiers until it was dropped onto the castle's walls at the moment of attack.

The ship was steered close to the shore with oars.

▼ A VIKING LONGSHIP

The Vikings were fierce warriors and excellent navigators. The kind of ship they used for war, which we call a longship, they called a *drakkar*. This meant "dragon," after the dragon head that was often carved on the **prow** of the ship.

Viking Raids

The Viking **longship** is the best-known medieval ship. The Vikings were a fierce warrior people from Scandinavia. They were feared because of their murderous attacks along the coasts of Western Europe from the 700s to the 900s. Longships were built of overlapping planks of wood. They were narrow, open ships that could be either rowed by hand or powered by sail. They allowed Vikings to make a quick getaway after raiding European kingdoms of wealth.

The mere sight of a Viking ship spread fear along European shores. The Vikings even sailed their longships up the Seine

The **keel** allowed longships to sail in a straight direction over long distances.

Oars were used when there was not enough wind.

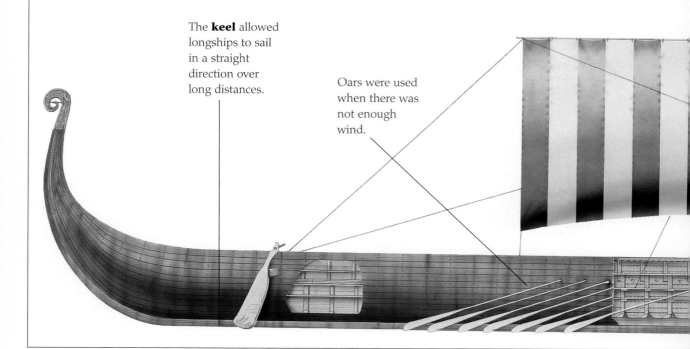

River in 885 and attempted to capture Paris, France. King Charles paid the Vikings a huge **ransom** to sail away and leave the city unharmed.

Naval Crusades

Ships transported Christian armies during the Crusades. They carried several Crusader armies across the Adriatic Sea, between present-day Italy and Greece, saving them a long march over land.

The mast was taken down in high winds so it would not break.

The sail was made of wool or **linen** pieces that were carefully stitched together.

A dragon's head was carved on the ship's prow.

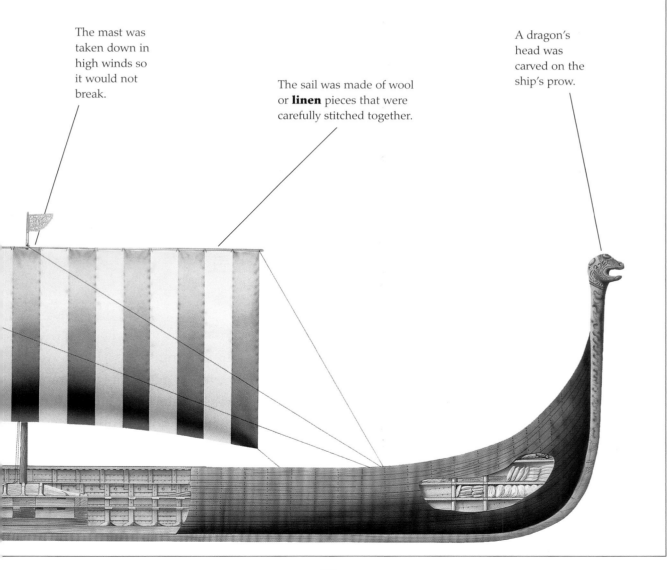

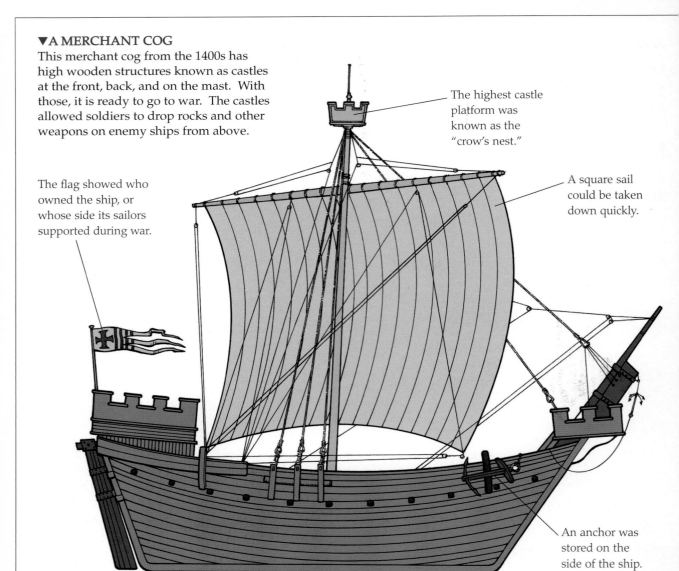

▼A MERCHANT COG
This merchant cog from the 1400s has high wooden structures known as castles at the front, back, and on the mast. With those, it is ready to go to war. The castles allowed soldiers to drop rocks and other weapons on enemy ships from above.

The highest castle platform was known as the "crow's nest."

The flag showed who owned the ship, or whose side its sailors supported during war.

A square sail could be taken down quickly.

An anchor was stored on the side of the ship.

Medieval Cogs

By the 1100s, a tall ship called a **cog** was in wide use in northern Europe. A cog had a single mast and a square sail. It stood about 13 feet (4 m) above the water. Cogs were often used by merchants, but were taken over by rulers when they were needed in times of war. The cog's flat bottom made sailing up rivers and getting close to the shore easy. That was useful when attacking a city.

Tactics at Sea

In ship-to-ship fighting in the Middle Ages, commanders tried to get as close to an enemy ship as possible. That allowed them to rain down weapons, including arrows, spears, and Greek fire, into the other ships. Taller ships had an advantage, as crews could drop heavy objects into the other ships. Men threw rocks to damage both crew and ship. They also threw a

▲ TRANSPORTING A MEDIEVAL ARMY
This illustration from the 1500s shows English soldiers arriving to aid the Duke of Brittany during the Hundred Years' War. The banners show the English lions on red and the fleur-de-lis (FLUR-de-LEE), the French flower symbol, on blue.

dangerous powder called quicklime to blind the ship's crew. They tossed anything they could get, including jars of soap. Soap made the deck slippery and dangerous for men and horses.

A fight at sea was often won by boarding the enemy ship and murdering its crew. The victors could then take over the ship and use it as their own. Attackers tried to capture enemy ships without sinking them because they were so valuable.

Onboard Weapons

The most effective weapon on board a ship was the crossbow. It could be shot from far away to kill the enemy's men before getting close enough for hand-to-hand combat.

The first recorded gun on a ship was installed on an English cog in the 1330s. The gun shot lead pellets and crossbow bolts. Although guns were gradually added to most ships, they were only light guns. If large guns were fired from deck, the force of the shot could sink the ship!

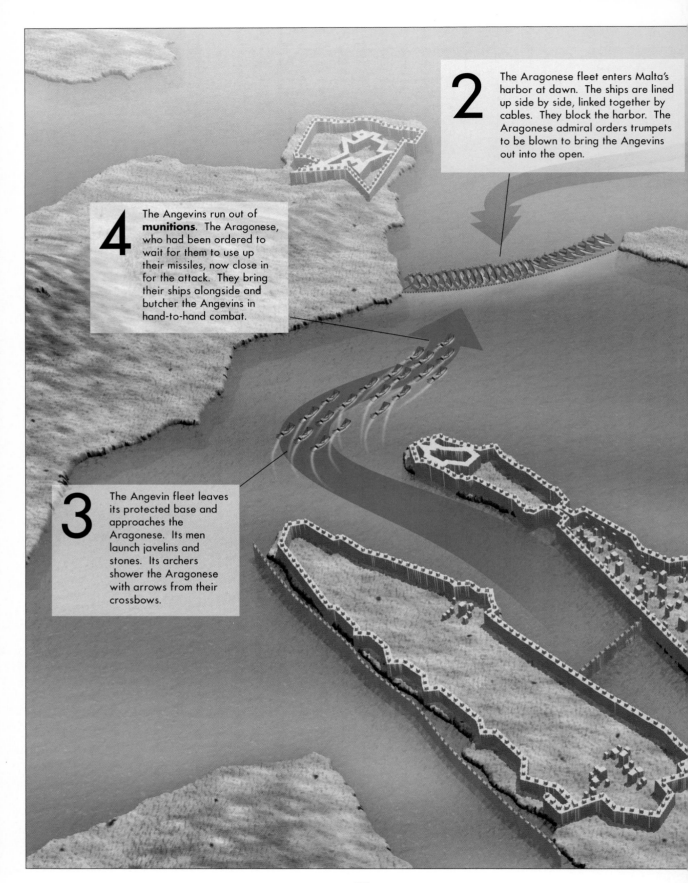

2 The Aragonese fleet enters Malta's harbor at dawn. The ships are lined up side by side, linked together by cables. They block the harbor. The Aragonese admiral orders trumpets to be blown to bring the Angevins out into the open.

4 The Angevins run out of **munitions**. The Aragonese, who had been ordered to wait for them to use up their missiles, now close in for the attack. They bring their ships alongside and butcher the Angevins in hand-to-hand combat.

3 The Angevin fleet leaves its protected base and approaches the Aragonese. Its men launch javelins and stones. Its archers shower the Aragonese with arrows from their crossbows.

The Battle of Malta
June 8, 1283

The island of Malta, south of Italy in the Mediterranean Sea, was the scene of one of the greatest sea battles of the 1200s. It was part of a war between the Duke of Anjou, now a part of present-day France, and King Pedro III of Aragon, a region of Spain. They both wanted to rule the Kingdom of Sicily, which included southern Italy and the island of Sicily itself.

The Duke of Anjou's forces, known as the Angevins (An-JEV-ins), were occupying the harbor at Malta. Their ships were smaller than the Aragonese (Ar-uh-gone-EASE) warships, which were the latest designs with tall platforms on the front and back. The Aragonese also had better-trained fighters and more experienced **admirals**. The inexperienced Angevin admirals had been given their commands because their fathers had held them previously, rather than because they were the best men for the job. That was a bad way to pick military commanders. Medieval sea battles could not be won without cunning tactics and well-trained sailors.

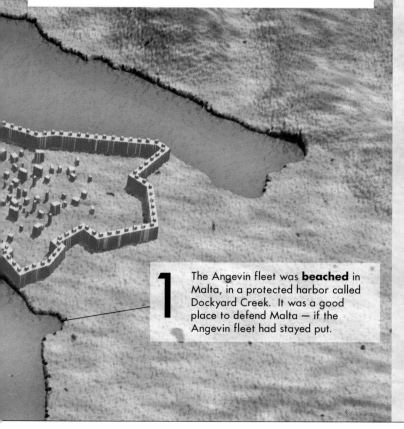

▲ AN ONBOARD CROSSBOW

Ships rarely had built-in weapons like this crossbow. Soldiers normally carried their own weapons. In special cases, crossbows were fitted to a stand to keep them steady when firing at sea.

1 The Angevin fleet was **beached** in Malta, in a protected harbor called Dockyard Creek. It was a good place to defend Malta — if the Angevin fleet had stayed put.

Glossary

admirals—commanders of fleets of ships

allies—people fighting on the same side against a common enemy

Basque—the native people of an area on the borders of present-day France and Spain

beached—dragged ashore

bribing—offering money secretly or illegally in return for information or help

cavalry—soldiers who are trained to fight on horseback

cog—type of medieval merchant ship with a single mast and a square sail

crossbows—small bows with instruments for drawing strings and releasing arrows

Franks—a western European Germanic group who became powerful during the early Middle Ages and whose territory included northern France, Belgium, and western Germany

heralds—official messengers who carried orders between a king and his nobles on the battlefield

infantry—soldiers who are trained and armed to fight on foot

javelins—light spears used as weapons and thrown by hand

keel—the central part of a ship or boat running along its bottom

linen—cloth woven from the flax plant

longbows—large bows drawn by hand and used to shoot arrows

longship—a type of long, narrow wooden sailing ship used by the Vikings

men-at-arms—well-trained and well-armed soldiers who were usually paid to fight

munitions—weapons and the objects that can be thrown or shot from them, including arrows and cannon balls

nobles—members of the wealthy ruling class

pagan—a person who does not believe in a single god but instead worships a number of nature gods or spirits

peasants—poor people who lived and worked on a lord's land in return for a share of the food produced

pilgrims—religious people who travel to a place or shrine important to their faith

prow—the pointed front of a ship's bow above the water

quiver—a case for holding arrows

ransom—money or valuables given to a person or group in exchange for safety

scouts—people who instructed soldiers on the battlefield and gave messages to troops

sheath—a covering for a blade such as a dagger or sword

steppes—huge grass-covered plains in Europe and Asia

tactics—the strategies and techniques used during war or battle

tunic—a loose, thigh-length piece of clothing similar to a dress, often without sleeves

For More Information

Books

The Bayeux Tapestry. David Mackenzie Wilson (Thames & Hudson, 2004)

Knights, Castles, and Warfare in the Middle Ages. World Almanac Library of the Middle Ages (series). Fiona MacDonald (World Almanac Library, 2005)

Medieval Life. Eyewitness Books (series). (DK Publishing, 2004)

Medieval Warfare. Medieval World (series). Tara Steele (Crabtree Publishing, 2003)

Medieval Weapons and Warfare: Armies and Combat in Medieval Times. The Library of the Middle Ages (series). Paul Hilliam (Rosen, 2004)

The Norman Conquest of England. Pivotal Moments in History (series). Janice Hamilton (Twenty-First Century Books, 2007)

Web Sites

Castle & Siege Terminology
http://home.olemiss.edu/~tjray/medieval/castle.htm
Search a glossary of terms that describes the features of medieval castles and fortresses. Find out about turrets, parapets, weapons, and much more.

Castles of Britain: Castle Learning Center
http://www.castles-of-britain.com/castle6.htm
Tour this fascinating site. It contains articles, photographs, artwork, and diagrams explaining medieval life, including information about castles and weaponry.

Kidipede—History for Kids
http://www.historyforkids.org/learn/medieval/history/history.htm
Explore this site that features historical essays about life during the Middle Ages with art, video clips, and reading suggestions.

The Medieval World: Medieval Battles
http://medieval.etrusia.co.uk/battles
Learn more about medieval England, its castles, knights, warfare, and the Crusades.

The Middle Ages
http://www.learner.org/interactives/middleages
Charge through this site and learn about the feudal system, religion, castles, clothing, and the arts.

Index